The Flowering Quince Poetry Series: Number Six

Edward Kleinschmidt

TO REMAIN

The Heyeck Press: Woodside 1990

© Edward Kleinschmidt 1990   ISBN 0-940592-24-x

I would like to thank T.R. Hummer, editor of *New England Review* where "To Remain" will appear in the Winter 1991 issue. Also, thanks to Steve Privett, S.J., for his documents on El Salvador. And to Frances Mayes, for her advice on the poem.

November sixteenth, nineteen eighty-nine,
In San Salvador, the unsaved city,
The soldiers rephrase *Genesis*: Let there be

Light, so we can see those we're killing,
The right bodies or the wrong bodies.
The death squad posters say, *Be a Patriot,*

Kill a Priest. And on this night the Atlacatl
Battalion, accents of training drills at Fort
Benning, Georgia, still in their ears, MADE

IN THE U.S.A. bullets in their belts, circle
The University of Central America. Inside the gates,
They drag five Jesuits from their cots, men who

Yesterday said masses for the massacred, their
Minds now reminded of no new future testament.
They are now face down, fatherly eyes in the dust

Of the courtyard. And according to the official
Report, the bodies are lined from north to south
With their heads toward the west, and their feet

Stretched toward the east. And after the killing,
After the commander's simple words, "Let's proceed,"
There remains Amando López, 55, theology professor,

Found in the following position: head to the west,
Feet pointed to the east, mouth down, left arm bent
Toward the west, right arm bent to the east, dressed

In striped shorts, green poncho, green jeans. And easily
Found next to him, there remains Ignacio Martín Baró, 46,
Psychology professor and Vice-Rector, found in

The following position: head to the west, feet
To the east, left arm to the west, right arm bent
To the north, right foot on the left foot, mouth

Down, wearing a blue shirt, black leather belt, gray
Pants, black shoes and socks. And Segundo Montes, 56,
Sociology professor and Director of Human Rights, who

Had said, "I want to live with the people who suffer
And deserve more," found in the following position:
Mouth down, feet extended to the northeast, head

To the southwest, left arm and right arm bent
Below the head with direction to the south,
Wearing beige shorts, beige shirt, and green jeans.

And next to him, Ignacio Ellacuría, 59,
University Rector, mouth down, head to the north,
Feet to the south, left arm to the north, right

Arm bent toward the face, wearing a brown bathrobe,
Beige shorts with vertical stripes, blue shoes. And
Next to him Juan Ramón Moreno, 55, theology professor,

Found in the following position: mouth down, head
To the east, feet to the west, arms extended toward
The southwest, dressed in black corduroy pants, black

Belt, long-sleeved blue shirt, purple shorts, brown
Leather shoe on the right foot. And inside
The residence, one remaining priest, called Lolo,

Joaquin López y López, 71, Director of *Fé y Alegría*
The quiet one, who was chased through the corridors,
Found in the following position: mouth up, head

To the east, feet to the west, arms bent over
The chest, hands semi-closed, wearing a white sleeveless
Undershirt, brown pants, black belt, shorts with vertical

Stripes. And in the room off the kitchen, where they asked
To spend the night to escape the night of city violence,
Of quiet killings done quickly, the new siege, civilians

Beholding that one brightest star exploding, as their
Roofs are torn off by bombs, children watching
Fire fights after curfew through cracks in the walls,

In this room, Elba Julia Ramos, 40, Jesuit Community cook,
Mouth up, head to the north, left foot to the south and right
Foot to the southwest, right arm to the northwest, left arm

To the southeast, both extended, wearing a blue dress, beige
Slip, black leather shoes, white bra; and her daughter,
Celina Ramos, 15, high school student, mouth up, head to the north,

Feet to the south, right arm over the chest, left arm
Perpendicular to the left side with direction to the north,
Wearing blue shorts, black, orange, red, and beige vertically

Striped blouse, white leather shoes with laces. Elba and Celina,
Who were "rekilled" when heard moaning from wounds, were
Found embracing before the M-16 fired ten more bullets

Into their bodies. And Elba was discovered that morning
By her husband at the same moment that Celina was discovered
That morning by her father, a *campesino* who cannot

Write this down, but instead weeks later planted two white rose
Bushes in the courtyard, one for Elba, one for Celina,
And surrounded them with six red rose bushes, one to the north,

One to the south, one to the east, one to the west, cardinal
Points, and two to directions that haven't been invented yet,
A compass of roses that searches for where we are going,

That can tell us where we have been. The white bushes
Are like the needle in the compass that tries to point
Beyond compassion. Or to tell us who the third person left

Standing is, the one who sees all, the witness, the one
Who has testimony, who has lamentation, who stands in
For the 70,000 Salvadoreans killed in one decade.

Edward Kleinschmidt's second book of poems, *First Language*, was awarded the 1989 Juniper Prize from The University of Massachusetts Press. The Heyeck Press published his first book of poems, *Magnetism*, which received the 1988 Poetry Award from the San Francisco Bay Area Book Reviewers Association.

His poems have appeared in many journals and anthologies, including *The American Poetry Review*, *The Gettysburg Review*, *The New Yorker*, *Poetry* (Chicago), *Virginia Quarterly Review*, and *The Best American Poetry, 1990*, among others.

He teaches English and Creative Writing at Santa Clara University, where he is an Assistant Professor.

"To Remain" received the 1990 Gesu Award in Poetry, sponsored by the Jesuit Institute for the Arts and by Alpha Sigma Nu, the national Jesuit Honor Society.

To Remain was designed, set, and printed by Robin Heyeck, with Centaur and Arrighi type on Mohawk Superfine paper. She printed the edition of 950 on a Chandler Price platen press between November 27 and December 16, 1990. Two hundred copies were bound in Heyeck hand marbled paper.

The Heyeck Press: 25 Patrol Court, Woodside, CA 94062

NORMANDALE COMMUNITY COLLEGE
LIBRARY
9700 FRANCE AVENUE SOUTH
BLOOMINGTON, MN 55431-4399